ESSENTIAL
SHAKER
STYLE

ESSENTIAL
SHAKER
STYLE

TESSA EVELEGH

WARD LOCK

A WARD LOCK BOOK

First published in the UK 1995
by Ward Lock
Wellington House
125 Strand
LONDON
WC2R0BB

A Cassell Imprint

First paperback edition 1998
Reprinted 1998

Distributed in the United States
by Sterling Publishing Co., Inc.
387 Park Avenue South, New York,
NY 10016-8810

A British Library Cataloguing in
Publication Data block for this book
may be obtained from the British
Library

ISBN 0-7063-7749-4

Designed by Nick Clark
Illustrations by Sally Launder
Printed and bound in Spain by
Bookprint S.L.
Front cover photograph:
Michael Freeman
Back cover photograph:
The Recollections Furniture
Company

$\mathcal{C}$ONTENTS

$\mathcal{I}$NTRODUCTION

WHERE DESIGN MEETS LIFESTYLE

Whatever your personal style, a priority when decorating and furnishing your home is very likely to be that you want to make it a peaceful and relaxing place. And perhaps, nowadays, this has become even more paramount. The ever-increasing pace of life, with international travel and Internet communications serving to make our lives faster rather than easier, is creating even greater expectations of how much can be fitted into a day. So much more, then, when we close our doors, do we need a peaceful haven. This is one reason why Shaker style has become so popular in recent times. Its elegant lines, uncluttered by pattern and embellishment, offer an atmosphere of calm and order.

It is a style, developed and perfected over 200 years at an unhurried pace, that transcends commercialism. Its aim was never to make money. Its aim was no less than perfection, initially from a purely practical point of view. But, in aiming for efficiency, even everyday items often acquire proportions that are easy on the eye; a tool delicately balanced for use, a box with a perfectly fitting lid, a chair designed to support the human frame – these all take on a harmony that is naturally pleasing. Having attained those heights of functional design, the Shakers went on to perfect the lines from a visual standpoint. 'Beauty rests on utility,' they believed, and 200 years of working on that philosophy has proved them right. Even if their style is not to everyone's taste (and certainly, during the last century when embellishment seemed to be all-important, many found Shaker designs impossibly plain), nobody can question the quality of the design.

To really understand Shaker style, it is important to understand the people and their lifestyle because the way they decorated their homes and the way they perfected everything they made ran much deeper than ordinary design. It ran into a whole expression of their spirituality. Understanding this does not have to be as lofty as it sounds. We do not have to emulate the Shaker

'Beauty in utility' was the Shaker catchphrase that demanded that everything they made was first and foremost functional and, second, that it carried an inherent beauty. Even the knobs on this highly efficient storage system are arranged with precision to make it more visually pleasing.

lifestyle to inherit the legacy of their design and the benefits of peaceful, harmonious surroundings. But, without understanding them and their ideals, it is very easy to become sidetracked. Realizing the appeal of Shaker design, many manufacturers have jumped on the bandwagon for commercial gain, labelling goods as Shaker style which go quite against Shaker principles. Understanding those principles will give you an instinctive feel for what is right and an infinitely more pleasing finished effect.

So, to write about Shaker style has to be more than simply about design. It is as much to do with writing about a very particular, very puritan religious group of people, who were established in the late 18th century and who saw work as a prayer, and perfection in the eyes of God as their goal. The generations of work that went into their designs mean they carry a depth of beauty that would be difficult to match in a one-off piece.

8 *Exquisitely made Shaker boxes have become an icon of Shaker design. Generally made by the Elders, their proportions were refined to an outstanding gracefulness. The attention to detail demonstrates the Shaker belief that 'Trifles make perfection but perfection is no trifle'.*

'Whatever is fashioned, let it be plain and simple and for the good,' instructed their founder, Mother Ann Lee. But that was not to say they were to be unconcerned about the look of their work: 'If it is both useful and necessary,' they held, 'don't hesitate to make it beautiful as long as the decorative elements are inherent in the design and don't interfere with function.' By shunning all kinds of decoration, the materials and designs had to work harder. There were no patterns or trims to disguise incongruous lines or shoddy workmanship.

The reason the Shakers were able to produce such fine designs, produced to such high standards, was that they freed themselves of many of the contraints of modern life. Their mixed but celibate communal life meant there were plenty of hands for plenty of jobs – some were allocated to dealing with the distracting minutiae of life, such as paying bills, cleaning, cooking and working the land; others spent their days in the workshops, working, as they were exhorted to by Mother Ann, 'as if they had a thousand years to live, and as if they were to die tomorrow', giving each piece as much time as it needed to produce a quality they could be pleased with.

The Shakers were not in the least competitive, and all aimed to work for the common good. Where one was slower, another was faster, and all benefited. This was recognized by Father Joseph Meacham, one of the early leaders, who said: 'From each according to his ability, to each according to his need'.

The combination of this goal of perfection and the fact that each piece was further refined by generation upon generation of Shakers led to beautifully proportioned, functional designs that are a pleasure to use and a delight to behold. Teamed together within a room, decorated in much the same way as those the Shakers may have lived in, it produces a pleasing harmony.

Because the Shakers were celibate, yet lived communally in 'dwelling houses', they did not have all the rooms we would expect to have in modern family houses. It is hardly unexpected that they did not have proper bathrooms – washstands with a bowl and jug sufficed. This was normal, even in what they would have seen as the 'outside world' in the 18th and much of the 19th century. Also not surprisingly, bearing in mind that they were celibate, was the lack of private bedrooms. Instead, the Shakers slept in small single-sex dormitories that they called 'retiring rooms'. A little more surprising to us in the outside world, was the lack of living rooms. They had no need; their time was filled with worship and work. However, this does not make their style irrelevent to our lifestyles. By understanding Shaker design – natural materials, natural colours and elegant forms – you can make the right choices when selecting modern equivalents to create a harmonious look throughout the room, or even house. For example, the Shakers never had upholstered furniture, but we can create a harmony by choosing the right colours and fabrics in a simple, plain design that has elegant sweeping lines. The same applies to the bathroom. With their meticulous attention to cleanliness, the Shakers would doubtless have had very efficient bathrooms, had the plumbing of the time allowed. By applying typical Shaker elements to a modern bathroom, we can be sure the finished effect will be one that even Mother Ann would have approved.

CHAPTER ONE

THE SHAKERS: A BRIEF HISTORY

THE SHAKER STORY BEGINS in the middle of 18th-century England when James and Jane Wardley founded the United Society of Believers in Christ's Second Appearing. They became known as the Shakers because of the powerful influence of the Holy Spirit during worship, which led to frantic movements such as dancing, swirling, flapping, shaking, or simply writhing on the floor. Late 18th-century authorities found this most unsettling and, in 1770, imprisoned one of the followers, Ann Lee, for disturbing the Sabbath. It was while Ann Lee was in prison that she had a vision for a new way of life that would allow people to live in a society where everyone was equal, regardless of age, sex, colour or race, and free from violence, war, greed and lust. Since she saw greed and sex as responsible for most of the world's problems, this would be a celibate society that could work together for the good of all rather than for financial gain.

THE FIRST SHAKERS

An illiterate textile worker and wife of a blacksmith, Ann Lee seemed an unlikely candidate to lead a religious sect to America. But, in 1774, a small group that included Ann, her husband, her younger brother William, and James Whittaker, a distant cousin, set off for New York.

The first six years were very hard. Ann's husband left her, their attempt to build a communal house came to nothing when it burned down and, in that time, they had had no converts in America. But, in 1780, a revival swept through America, and numbers began to grow.

Ann was not destined to see the true flowering of Shakerism as she died four years later, weakened by imprisonment, a tough schedule and grief at the death of her brother, William. Her successor, James Whittaker, who came with the group from England, kept the believers together for another three years until he was succeeded by Baptist minister Joseph Meacham, one of the first Americans to join the Shakers, and Lucy Wright.

It was Joseph Meacham and Lucy Wright who set up the

utopian communal Shaker villages, giving the Shakers the freedom to pursue their goals and set up farms and workshops.

The first village was established in 1787 at New Lebanon, New York, when about 100 believers moved into a group of small farms, bringing all their belongings for communal use. By 1794, there were 11 communities all across New England, organized into several 'families'. Each family lived in a dwelling house grouped around a meeting house where they gathered for worship. The most senior house was called Church House; the others were named by their location in relation to the meeting house, such as North Family, South Family, East Family, or by a geographical feature, such as Hill Family, or their occupation, such as Mill Family. The families were not blood families as we know them, although some whole families did join the Shakers, bringing their children with them. In these instances, the husbands lived in the Brethren's quarters, the wives with the Sisters, and the children were housed separately. However, the Shaker system was different to most celibate communities in that the sexes were mixed within the dwelling houses, one side of

The bell-pull at the centre of this landing formed the dividing line between the Brethrens' retiring rooms (dormitory-like bedrooms) to the left, and the Sisters' retiring rooms to the right.

which was set aside for the Brethren, and the other for the Sisters. While they had social union meetings, in which the men and women got together several times a week, this was arranged on a rota system, so that individuals did not have the opportunity to become close.

Within the families was a system of leadership: two Elders and two Eldresses were responsible for the spiritual well-being of the family; two Deacons and Deaconesses dealt with the practical matters, such as work schedules, laundry, meals, allocating of clothing, tools and furnishings; and four trustees, two of each sex, dealt with the business side of living, such as bills and dealings with the outside world. The Shakers lived for the good of all, sharing everything. Although celibacy meant there was no natural replacement, this system did mean that everyone was there of their own volition, and had a commitment to the system.

SHAKER LIFESTYLE

Work was always very much a part of the Shakers' lifestyle. The original band of followers who came over from England were working class: Ann herself had worked in the textile mills, her brother was a blacksmith, and James Whittaker was a weaver. 'Put your hands to work and your hearts to God,' Mother Ann urged her followers, so every act became a form of spiritual worship as they aspired to perfection.

The Shakers' first task was to coax their meagre land into enough production to provide sufficient food for the community. In the early days they lived on little more than porridge and bread made from rye and Indian meal. Over the years, they increased both the productivity and the size of their farms until there was more than enough for their own needs, and they were able to sell their produce. The same applied to the furniture, fabrics, tools and utensils they made for their own daily needs. Generally, the Shakers made items in batches so that, for example, everyone could have a new chair at the same time, rather than a privileged few. This translated well when the Shakers started to produce items for sale.

Once a system was perfected, some Brethren could work at a fantastic rate. When making brooms one Brother, Orren Haskins, turned 1000 handles in a day in 1836, although this was seen as something of a record, even at the time.

Soon the Shakers had a surplus that they could sell – not for commercial gain, but to help with living costs. They started to sell their ladder-back chairs quite early on, in 1792. By their hey-day at the end of the 19th century, they were manufacturing endless items for sale: textiles, including their famous homespun cotton, pure wool and linens; they were also one of the first communities to sell seeds; and they grew herbs and flowers for culinary, pharmaceutical and cosmetic purposes. At their peak, the Shaker communities cultivated 240 different types of herbs, many of which were sold to the outside world. They supplemented their own herbal knowledge with techniques gleaned from the local Indians about the properties of local plants and, later, they collaborated with doctors from the outside world to increase their skills in contemporary medicine. The herbs that were to be sold for medicinal purposes were compressed into hard cakes of varying sizes. These cakes were wrapped in coloured paper for distribution all over America, and even export to Europe where they earned a high reputation for quality.

Everything the Shakers made both for themselves and for sale carried a hallmark of quality. For them, nothing less than perfection was good enough. Every detail in everything they did was scrutinized. 'Trifles make perfection, but perfection is no trifle,' they said. The knowledge that the Shakers always worked in an honest way and to the highest standards made their goods much in demand. However, their modest lifestyle and personal bearing did not put them above rigorous advertising campaigns in which they boasted the quality of their products.

As well as simply selling their own surpluses, the Shakers developed lines that were only for sale to the outside world. These were items that they certainly would never have used, such as cosmetics, distilled flower waters, decorative herbal gifts, lined

baskets, sewing boxes and other 'fancy goods'. But they were nevertheless made from materials they had produced themselves and to the same high standards.

Although the Shakers chose to live a pure and simple life, they were not closed to progress in the outside world. Their pharmaceuticals benefited from collaboration with medical doctors outside the community; the productivity of their farms was improved with the help of contemporary technology, which was often further improved by the Shakers themselves.

Since the Shakers were drawn from every area of the outside community, they brought with them endless skills – farming, building, carpentry, spinning, weaving, blacksmithing, basket-making, shoe making, dentistry, medicine and surgery. Each worked hard to attain perfection in his or her own area, but that certainly did not preclude him or her from other skills. 'If you improve in one talent,' they believed, 'God will give you more'.

COMMUNAL WORK

The seasons dictated the Shakers' work, taking the men and boys outside in the summer to work the fields, and bringing them into the workshops or school in the winter. For the Sisters, summer meant food preservation – the drying of herbs, bottling of fruit, making of jams, and manufacturing of dyes, while the girls attended school. In the winter, they all spun, wove textiles, and made baskets and fancy goods. Even this simple diversity of work according to the seasons together with rotas in the kitchens or woodyard meant that all Shakers were skilled in more than one area. Some, like Giles Avery, were extraordinarily versatile. He turned his hand to masonry, plumbing, carpentry, plastering, teaching, cabinet-making, farming and writing. Evidently one of the most gifted Shakers, he eventually became an Elder.

Untypical of their era, Shakers believed in complete equality between the Sisters and the Brethren. Although they did divide the work by gender, this was mainly to avoid too much contact between the sexes, and so threaten their celibate society.

Opposite: Sisters generally enjoyed the convivial atmosphere of the kitchens. They usually worked four-week rotas, preparing three meals a day for up to 100 members of the community.

To ensure that their communal life ran smoothly, the Shakers were extremely organized. Their days were run to a strict schedule, rotas were organized and jobs were allocated according to the needs of the community and the season.

Shaker Sisters worked in the kitchen on four-week shifts. It was work they seemed to look forward to: the ovens kept the room warm and, working in teams, the atmosphere was generally sociable. The workload was immense: one record stated that they made a total of 620 pies in one month. Another sister reported plucking 35 chickens after breakfast. In their kitchen gardens, they cultivated an abundance of vegetables and herbs for their own table, with enough left over for visitors to dine on a lavish lunch for a meagre 25 cents.

Each group of Sisters developed their own recipes, serving up a deliciously varied diet to the group. Meat, poultry and fresh young vegetables were delicately flavoured with herbs straight from the kitchen garden. For pudding, they made mouthwatering fruit pies topped with crisp pastry. In later years, the food was transported from the kitchens up to the dining room in dumb waiters; these worked on a pulley system that ensured the food arrived while it was still hot. These dumb waiters soon became a common feature of Shaker dwelling houses.

SHAKER FURNISHINGS

The lifestyle of the Shakers governed their material needs, and this contributed greatly to the decoration of their dwelling houses and design of their furniture. Everyone could be more comfortably seated if tables were larger than the average domestic one. They were usually 3m (10ft) long with breadboard ends, which allowed for expansion during damp weather. They were given trestle legs with a brace along their length to allow plenty of leg room for all. Chairs were designed with ladder-backs so they could be conveniently hung up on the peg rail while the floor was swept. They were lightweight and they had pommels or finials at the top so they could be easily lifted.

Storage had to be well considered: the Shakers did not want to waste time looking for things. 'Provide places for all your things,' said Mother Ann, 'so that you may know where to find them at any time, day or night'. But communal living meant that there was an additional reason for order in storage: many things were shared and everyone had to have access to them. For example, in the work-shops, tools had to be available to all. 'When anyone borrows a tool,' dictated the Millenial Laws of 1841, which governed the running of the communities, 'it should be immediately returned without injury, if possible...The wicked borrow and never return.' The Shakers knew that good storage was the root of an ordered life.

They were also meticulous about cleaning: 'There is no dirt in Heaven,' reasoned Mother Ann. This combination of needing plenty of storage that was easy to clean around led to the Shaker preference for built-in furniture that reached from floor to ceiling to exclude dust traps. This is all relevent to our very different lives today. Small living spaces demand hardworking storage – a need that has been met by many manufacturers who now produce endless ranges of built-in kitchen and bedroom furniture.

The peg rail, too, was a most useful hanging system that they recessed into walls throughout their dwelling and meeting houses at picture rail level. More than just coat hooks, the pegs were used to hang furniture, small cupboards, candle-holders, wall cloths for insulation, tools, brushes, mirrors, and anything else that could possibly be hung up – both for easy access, and to get everything off the floor for cleaning.

In the golden age of Shakerism, during the mid-19th century, 6000 Brethren and Sisters lived this ordered life, giving their hearts to God and their hands to work. Since the Shakers were celibate, nobody was born into it, though the children who were either brought with families or were adopted from broken families had the opportunity to make their own commitment after they were 21 years old. The communities were not worried about their numbers, they were more concerned with the sincerity of each member. This was in no doubt in the early days when joining meant hardship. But,

as the Shakers prospered, so they attracted some people who were seeking security rather than salvation.

However, as the years passed, the communities dwindled as the old Shakers died and fewer people of the outside world were attracted to join. Nowadays, only one small group remains: at Sabbathday Lake, Maine, though some villages, such as Hancock Village and Canterbury, New Hampshire, have been restored and are now run as working museums, complete with craftspeople who demonstrate the traditional Shaker crafts.

Although the number of real Shakers is now less than a dozen,

The Shakers lived in dormitory-like retiring rooms, often sharing four to a room. The furnishings were rudimentary; everyone had a bed, a rug and some storage space.

even Mother Ann would not have regrets if she were still alive. She had a vision that when there were as many Shakers left as there are fingers on a child's hand, there would be another revival. Even now, there is a resurgence of interest in their design and style as both the recent demand for Shaker goods, and indeed this book, testify. And with that interest we can, perhaps, learn something about the Shakers' profound spirituality whose legacy can bestow us with a harmonious style of decorating and design for our homes that is still very relevant to modern living.

CHAPTER TWO
SHAKER STYLE:
THE SIX ESSENTIAL ELEMENTS

THERE IS SOMETHING UNIVERSALLY beguiling about Shaker style. The appeal is the exquisite combination of just a few colours, the purity of the designs, and the ease with which you can put the look together yourself. There are no complicated colour schemes to cope with, no tricky patterns to match, no clever curtain styles to master. There are just a few elements which repeat themselves again and again throughout the whole house. If you understand those elements and have an idea of Shaker philosophy, you can very quickly put together an elegant style that still offers room for your own expression. And, best of all, this is a look so beautifully developed over 200 years that it transcends fashion, and it does not date – witness the fact it has recently enjoyed a revival and looks graceful even in late 20th-century modern houses.

The basic elements that combine to produce an authentic Shaker look are: colour palette, fabrics, woodwork, furniture, storage and accessories.

COLOUR PALETTE

Walls in Shaker dwelling houses were invariably white plaster against which was set a very particular range of colours that was used both in paint and in textiles. The Shakers made most of the pigments and dyes themselves using local clays and plants, and the

The Shakers had a very distinctive colour palette, using dyes and pigments from the clays and plants around them. It ranged from pinky and terracotta earth shades, through yellow ochre and olive green, to greenish-blues and denim.

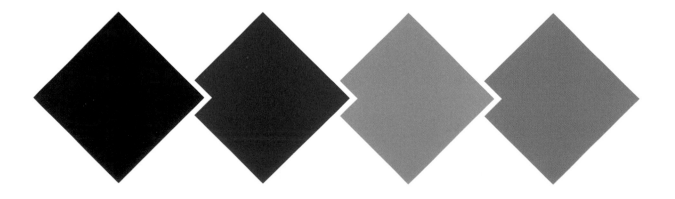

Shaker Sisters wove a wide variety of checked fabrics, all in the colours from their basic palette.

few that they bought in, indigo for example, were also derived from plant material. This resulted in wonderfully evocative shades that were harmonious because they came from nature. The palette ranged from pinky and terracotta earth shades, going through yellow ochres and olive greens to the bluish-greens, deep turquoises and, eventually, to the greenish-blues and denims. All the colours were strong, though they had a smudgy muted softness that took away any brashness. They worked well on their own and each looked good with any of the others. So, given this colour range, you can mix and match with assurance, and still know you will finish with a harmonious result.

FABRICS

Shaker Sisters made all their own fabrics, in pure natural fibres, including wool, cotton, flax and silk. They often began at the very beginning of the process by spinning and dyeing the wool or flax (for linen), before weaving the cloth. The cloth was frequently

There was plenty of woodwork in Shaker buildings, and it was often given a burnished gold-coloured stain, which brought a welcoming lightness to their rooms.

plain. The Shakers avoided patterns although, to lend relief to their otherwise plain interiors, they often wove checked fabrics. The checks themselves were many and varied – miniature ginghams, window checks, or checks that incorporated more than one colour. These fabrics were used for curtains, bedding and table linen. Some individual cloths, especially those that were used in the kitchen, were woven with fine striped borders.

WOODWORK

The Shakers featured a lot of woodwork in their interiors, and usually allowed the rich patterning of the woodgrain to show through a translucent orangey stain. Doors, floors, architraves, window frames, shutters, skirtings, peg rails at picture rail height, cupboards and whole walls of built-in wooden storage units all contributed to rooms with a predominantly timbered look. They chose exquisite fine-grained local woods, such as cherry and maple, which shone a brilliant marigold shade when varnished, and brought a vibrant light into the room. Occasionally, some of the woodwork – the window frames, perhaps, or the peg rail and skirting – was painted in one of their favourite shades.

Any accessories to woodwork, such as curtain rails and door furniture, were usually made of wrought iron.

The floor was always left as varnished timber (unless it was made of stone) and in some rooms, such as in retiring rooms where they were needed, simple woven wool or rag rugs were laid down.

FURNITURE

The fine wooden furniture, often made of cherry or maple and stained in the same way as the woodwork, was probably the best illustration of the Shaker belief that beauty rests on utility. They knew what every architecture and design student is now taught: that form follows function. By considering the function first, there is a harmony of balance that naturally 'looks right'. The piece can then be made to look even more beautiful by refining the lines into graceful curves. The Shakers felt it was important to perfect the

Furniture, such as this cherry settle, was made to elegant proportions with an extraordinary lightweight grace.

designs, continually improving the looks as long as there was no unnecessary embellishment. This offered a great challenge as, without the disguise of patterning or carving, incongruous lines or shoddy workmanship are shown up. So, eventually, the final pieces were honed to as near perfection both in their function and in their looks as is humanly possible. The classic Shaker ladder-back chair clearly demonstrates this, and moved one observer to comment: 'The peculiar grace of a Shaker chair is due to the maker's belief that an angel might come and sit on it.'

Ladder-back chairs were designed to be light – so they could easily be hung on the peg rail when the floor needed to be swept – with easy-grip pommel finials which made them simple to lift; yet they were designed to be strong to withstand the constant moving about. They had taped woven seats and backs that tilted slightly backwards for comfort. Their lines were refined to the extent that each rung of the ladder became narrower towards the top of the chair – simply to improve the visual appeal. As well as ladder-backs, the Shakers were comfortable with any honestly designed country chair such as the Windsor chair, as these were very likely to be the sort they brought with them when they joined the community.

Dining tables were usually of the trestle variety, to accommodate everyone comfortably, and there were innumerable side tables, often incorporating a single drawer. The legs were often slim and tapered, both to accommodate a respectably sized drawer, and to improve the looks. Round pedestal candle tables were another common feature in a Shaker dwelling house.

Since the Shakers did not really have leisure time as we know it – they were more likely to be in worship or social union meetings – they made little use of upholstery. However, it is not difficult to incorporate upholstery in keeping with the Shaker look, as long as you choose a simple, comfortable design that is covered in a plain or checked fabric in a colour from the Shaker palette.

STORAGE

An ordered communal life demands plenty of practical storage if everyone is to find what they need. The Shakers addressed this problem in a very similar way to the way we address it nowadays. By building in whole walls of storage from ceiling to floor, no space was wasted and all dust traps were excluded. The wall storage was often divided into units: cupboards and banks of drawers with handles were arranged in regimented lines for an ordered look. Drawers were designed to suit their contents. Some huge units consisted of scores of small square drawers, probably to hold herbs; others were made up of a single line of longer drawers that might have been gradated with the deeper ones at the bottom for heavier objects. These gradations were always finely executed to ensure visually pleasing proportions.

The other storage element that ran throughout all Shaker rooms, was the peg rail, which was recessed into every wall at picture rail level. It has become such a strong emblem of Shaker decoration that putting one up, even in a modern house, immediately lends Shaker style to any room. It is also incredibly useful. Anything that can be hung up can be put on these sturdy pegs. The Shakers themselves used them for coats, hats, walking sticks, small cupboards, chairs, mirrors, cleaning equipment, sconces and wall cloths for insulation. Nowadays, you may even like to add to this by hanging up decorative objects (though to fit with the purist Shaker philosophy, every object should have some use).

ACCESSORIES

Shakers would not tolerate anything that had no use, but even the most workaday items they made were bestowed with great beauty. Even a coathanger, made from a flat piece of wood that was exquisitely rounded at each end, had a grace that far outstretched its

Built-in storage would often run the whole length of a wall, and could be built up of several units of drawers and cupboards. The finished ensemble would always result in a visually pleasing arrangement.

function. And the classic Shaker storage boxes were refined to graceful oval proportions with elegant, finger-like swallowtail joins. Even in their day, they were expensive for what amounted to the equivalent of plastic storage boxes, but they were always in demand. Other accessories the Shakers had on display and used daily were simple metal candlesticks, candelabra, tin sconces, candle-boxes, basketware and brushes for sweeping. They also manufactured quality goods for sale to the outside world that did not fit in with their own stringent lifestyle, but did fit with their style in terms of materials and design. These might have included herbal and twiggy wreaths, rag dolls, sewing baskets, lavender sachets and cushions made from their homespun fabrics. These are all accessories that we, today, can include in our Shaker-style rooms, confident that they are in keeping with the look.

The Shakers would never have kept anything for pure ornamentation, but their everyday housewares carried an intrinsic beauty of their own. Arranged on a peg rail, they make decorative accessories while serving a useful purpose.

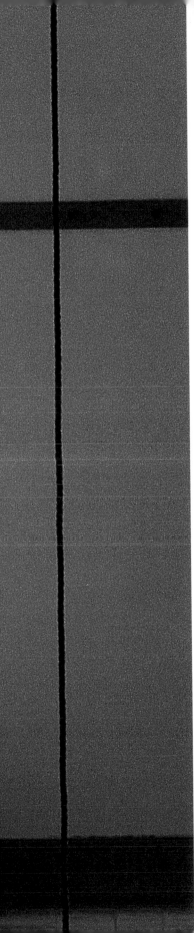

CHAPTER THREE

Halls and Stairways

A WARM, FRIENDLY WELCOME WAS ASSURED to everyone who stepped over a Shaker threshold. They were truly egalitarian, seeing everyone as equal in God's eyes regardless of colour, gender or race. This was quite extraordinary in 18th- and 19th-century America when women were definitely beholden to men and slavery was still in force. The harmonious style of Shaker decoration, reflected this egalitarianism, and was pleasing to every eye as it depended on natural materials and shunned unnecessary pattern and embellishment, thereby transcending taste.

STORAGE

The Shaker-style hall, as with all Shaker rooms, should be a very practical place, providing plenty of hanging and storage space. A peg rail running the full length of the hall offers ample hanging, not

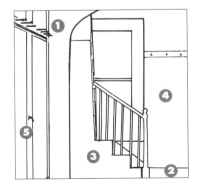

1 *Peg rail*
2 *Stone flooring*
3 *Natural wood stairway*
4 *Whitewashed walls*
5 *Wood cupboards with wrought iron door furniture*

Opposite: A ladder-back chair and candle table make for a convenient rest area in this hall. Where space is at a premium, the chair could be hung on the peg rail out of the way until needed.

only for all the family's coats, jackets and hats, but also for umbrellas, walking sticks, dog leads, even shoes or wellington boots if they are clipped together by a fastener with a hanging loop. You can also hang small cupboards onto the peg rail for storing small items, such as keys, well out of reach of small prying hands. Hanging a mirror from a hall peg rail could be very useful, too.

Another extremely practical idea worth imitating for the hall is to hang a ladder-back chair on the peg rail. Most of us have too little room in our halls to provide a permanent home for a chair, although they are very useful for taking off outdoor boots or shoes and, once the job is done, they can be hung conveniently out of the way.

If you have the space, build a floor-to-ceiling cupboard to provide ample storage so that everything can be tidied up out of the way. If there is very little room in the hallway, a cupboard could, perhaps, be fitted under the stairs. The Shaker look can be achieved by choosing one of their favourite woods, such as cherry or maple, or by staining a softwood to match. For an authentic look, the cupboards should be panelled. The original reason for this was that the frames provided strength, while thinner panels economized on wood. But absolutely no unnecessary mouldings are needed, so a graceful yet restrained look is achieved. Simple doorknobs or wrought iron furniture would finish off the Shaker look appropriately.

WALLS AND FLOORS

Whitewashed walls are typically Shaker, and these are especially suited to halls where light levels are low, and paler colours offer the best light reflection.

Hall floors can be laid with flagstones made from local material, quarry tiles, linoleum or bare softwood floorboards to match the peg rail. If you choose wood the floorboards, skirtings and peg rail, along with the stairway, can be given an orangey stain and waxed, or painted in one of the typical Shaker shades, such as rich earthy red, yellow ochre, olive or muted bluish-green.

32 *Tin sconces make attractive wall decorations, either singly, or hung in a group. Tin was commonly used; it was inexpensive, lightweight and easy to use.*

ACCESSORIES

There are many typically Shaker items that can be used to decorate the walls in a modern house. Tin candle sconces were part of everyday Shaker life, and they were made in many shapes; tall and thin, scooped, heart-shaped, and even mirrored to reflect extra light. Grouped together, these can make a delightful display. Everyday Shaker items, too, such as their exquisitely-made hand brushes, or candle-boxes for storing spare candles, can be appreciated for their beauty.

Given this uncluttered, elegant design and the efficient use of space and storage, modern hallways can offer the same harmonious welcome that those original Shaker dwelling houses projected, while perhaps affording a little extra space for necessary household activities that all too often get elbowed out. Work areas, for example, are needed in every home: somewhere to attend to the bills, paperwork from the school and other home correspondence. Finding room for this can be tricky in a modern space-hungry house. It might just be possible to steal a few hall-centimetres to install a neatly-designed Shaker desk. The Shakers perfected the art of making space-efficient desks, designing tall slim units with drop-down leaves and an abundance of storage space for files and papers both above and below the work area. Once the business is done, the leaf can be raised, leaving a neat wall-hugging unit that can be slipped into an alcove, onto the landing, or installed unobtrusively into the hallway itself.

The welcome of any home is not dependent on visual impact alone. The aroma it exudes has just as large a part to play. The woods and other building materials that are used will provide a part of the background perfume, which can be enhanced by the choice

of stains and waxes, and all the accessories around the house. In a Shaker-style home, you can recreate the typical aroma of beeswax candles and herbs by hanging candle-boxes containing beeswax candles on the peg rail, and making aromatic dried herb garlands that can be strung up alongside them.

This tall slimline desk with a fold-up top provides a surprising amount of storage space, yet can be accommodated in a narrow area.

BEESWAX CANDLES

Without the benefit of electricity, early Shakers relied heavily on candlelight, and much of their restrained style is represented in their elegant metal candlesticks, which were usually stood on the classic round candle tables all around the dwelling houses. Wall-hung tin candle sconces offered peripheral light, as did the wooden candle-holders designed especially to hang on the peg rail. However, safety laws dictated that lit candles could only be carried around in lanterns. Making your own beeswax candles is extremely simple if you use the specially made sheet beeswax.

You will need
❋

- Sheets of natural beeswax
- Scalpel or craft knife
- Ruler
- Candle wick

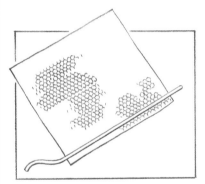

1 *Lay a sheet of natural beeswax on a flat surface. Using the ruler as a straight edge and a scalpel or craft knife, cut a rectangle of*

beeswax so the width is the desired length of the candle. Cut the wick to measure 3cm (1¼ in) longer

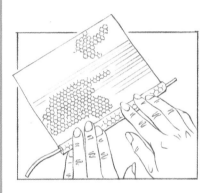

2 *Lay the wick onto the end of the wax rectangle, overlapping each edge, and carefully roll up the candle. The wax will stick to itself as you roll it. Trim the wick flush with the wax at one end.*

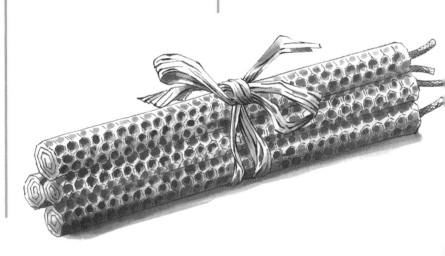

DRIED HERB GARLANDS

Most Shaker communities cultivated extensive herb gardens, drying the herbs both for culinary and pharmaceutical purposes. Much of the produce was sold to the outside world, and included dried herb garlands that they would have deemed unnecessary to their own lifestyle. However, they have a delightful aroma and make charming accessories that are very easy to assemble.

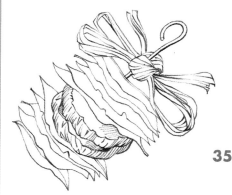

You will need
❋

- Heavy-gauge florist's wire
- Wire cutters
- Dried bay leaves
- Dried apple slices
- Raffia
- Scraps of checked fabric

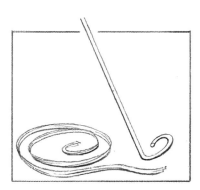

1 *Cut a piece of florist's wire the length of your desired decoration and make a loop in one end. Bend up the loop to make an L-shape.*

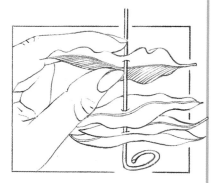

2 *Thread some dried bay leaves onto the wire and push down to the loop until you have a pile of about 3cm (1¼ in).*

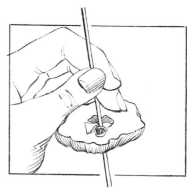

3 *Next, thread three or four dried apple slices onto the wire.*

4 *Thread on more bay leaves. Tie a hank of raffia to the top of the wire, if desired. Make a second loop at the top of the wire.*

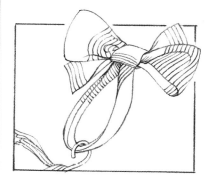

5 *Thread a strip of checked fabric through the top wire loop and make a fabric loop, tied at the top for hanging. Tie on a scrap of the same fabric at the bottom of the garland.*

CHAPTER FOUR

DINING ROOMS

THREE TIMES A DAY, THE TEMPTING AROMA of delicious home-grown produce cooking in delicately flavoured fresh herbs would waft up from the kitchen signalling meal times. The Shakers would gather together in the dining room, claiming their places on tape or rush-seated ladder-back chairs on either side of long, elegantly proportioned trestle tables. The ambience was a peaceful one, partly because they dined in silence, and partly due to the harmonious combination of white walls and fine wood furniture set with pure white china.

FURNITURE

Although practicality was always the Shakers' priority, this precluded neither beauty nor comfort. 'Whatever is fashioned,' instructed Mother Ann, 'let it be plain and simple and for the good'.

1 *Trestle dining table in solid maple or cherry wood*
2 *Rush-seated ladder-back chairs with easy-grip pommels*
3 *Natural wood flooring*
4 *Peg rail with hanging candlesticks*

5 *Storage cupboard for white ironstone crockery*
6 *Side table for serving*
7 *Whitewashed walls*
8 *Generously proportioned sash windows left bare*

No furniture demonstrates this better than Shaker dining furniture. The tables were built to graceful lines, often incorporating elegantly arched feet, but the trestle design was developed mainly so that everyone had plenty of leg room. The ladder-back chairs usually had seats of woven tapes, rather than rush, to make them more comfortable, and the back sloped gently backwards for easy sitting. Freed from the constraints of commercialism by their communal living, successive generations of Shakers were able to perfect the designs over the decades and centuries, leaving us a legacy of furniture so elegantly proportioned and finely balanced that it has universal appeal. Attention to detail was all: 'Trifles make perfection, but perfection is no trifle,' they were brought up to believe as they sought perfection in everything they did.

The attention to detail in the making of ladder-back chairs amply demonstrates this. The look of the furniture went beyond mere utility but, in aspiring to visual perfection, the Shakers relied on proportion and graceful lines, rather than the embellishment of carving or painting. Often the slats of the ladder-back chairs increased in width towards the top of the back to make them more pleasing to the eye. The front posts were made in one piece to provide strength, although a wooden disc would be glued on the top of the arm to make it easier to pull oneself out of the chair. At the back, many original Shaker chairs had tilter feet – small ball and socket joints fitted in place using a leather thong. This was the pragmatic result of being unable to stop Brethren and Sisters from leaning back on their chairs whose hardwood feet would cause damage to the softwood floors. It had obviously been a problem for some time as the Millenial Laws of 1821 admonished: 'It is not right to lean our chairs back,' yet, by 1830, tilter feet had become commonplace.

Even the distinctive pommels at the tops of Shaker chairs were there for a purpose. Shaker sisters would grasp these pommels and whisk the lightweight chairs up onto the peg rail after each meal to clear the floor for efficient sweeping. The dining chair seats were often made of tapes that the Shakers wove themselves. These were dyed in favourite Shaker shades including indigo blues, olive greens, ochre yellows and rust reds. Sometimes the seats were woven so the weft and warp tapes were of the same colour, to create a single colour seat. Sometimes, they were woven using contrasting tapes to create herringbone and chequerboard patterns.

All the chairs in the dwelling house were made to a similar design to the basic dining chair. However, some were given rockers, others had taped backs for comfort, while others had low backs, probably suited for sitting at work benches or clerical desks.

This reproduction dining table in cherry wood shows a typical Shaker trestle with arched feet.

40 *Reproduction Shaker ladder-back chairs in English cherry. As well as the classic tape-woven seats, many had rush seats like these. The tall back has wider slats at the top than the bottom — a detail the Shakers developed to perfect the visual appeal of the chair.*

WALLS

The general ambience of a classic Shaker-style dining room should be light and bright. The walls can be whitewashed and the woodwork either left natural or painted one of the Shakers' favourite muted earthy shades. However, if you frequently use your dining room for evening entertainment, when a more cosy atmosphere is demanded, choose pale shades of a light ochre, perhaps, or smudgy turquoise blue for the walls, and team it with woodwork picked out in darker tones. Add a peg rail, painted to match the rest of the woodwork to give the room true Shaker signature.

FABRICS

The Shakers tended to avoid curtains for dining room windows as they preferred plenty of natural light, and anything that inhibited it in any way for any reason other than modesty was to be avoided. They even designed internal windows into the walls so that light could pass through into or out of halls or passages. However, if you would prefer the privacy afforded by curtains, choose pure white cotton or checked homespun fabric for a Shaker feel. Curtains can have simple loop headings that do not demand fancy pinching or pleating, and be hung on simple metal poles.

Although Shakers did not use tablecloths, as they considered them an unnecessary embellishment, Shaker communities would

Although not classically Shaker, this dining room combines typical olive green shades with the simple design of a scrubbed wooden table, rush-seated chairs and bench seating.

Opposite: This modern interpretation of a Shaker dining room adds extra colour in classic Shaker green to the dining table and tape-seated ladder-back chairs. Homespun-style curtains have been added to afford some privacy.

certainly have had napkins. For an authentic look, choose napkins made of white or natural linen, or checked homespun fabric in white and blue, green or red. Linen was usually left plain and undecorated; however, cross stitch was used to work simple motifs onto linens for sale to the outside world. A favourite may have been a heart shape, representing Mother Ann's dictum: 'Put your hands to work and your hearts to God'.

Fresh checked linens could also be used to line Shaker baskets for serving bread. These baskets, which are still available today, were quite different from the woven willow that Mother Ann Lee would have recognized in her native Manchester. Instead of weaving the unsplit branch, the Shakers borrowed the technique of weaving with flat splints of wood from the local Algonquian Indians. They typically borrowed the rough original design and perfected it, to make the fine curved basketwork we have now come to regard as the Shakers' own. Even today, it is regarded by some as the finest splint basketwork ever seen.

ACCESSORIES

For an intimate evening atmosphere, add plenty of candlelight. A central wrought iron candelabra offers the perfect solution for the main lighting – you will be surprised at the light levels that 12 candles, all alight at once, can offer. This can be supplemented by sconces hung from the peg rail, in just the same way as the Shakers would have used them. Choose scented or aromatherapy candles to evoke the ambience of the changing seasons. Beeswax or pine lend a Christmassy feel, while in the summer you may like to choose lavender- or rose-scented candles.

A Shaker-style tray, characteristically made to ample and practical proportions, is another very useful accessory. Generously deep with integral handles, these trays made for steady carrying, while the splayed sides meant it was easy for servers to fit their hands comfortably into the handles, even when the trays were stacked high with crockery. The carved wooden rabbits also seen in the Shaker basket in the photograph (overleaf), are the sort of toys

44 *Wooden trays, platters, toys and homespun fabric embroidered with cross stitch tumble from a split-cane Shaker basket.*

the Brethren made in their workshops both for the children the Shakers adopted, and to sell in the outside world. Sisters also made appealing toys, such as rag dolls delightfully dressed in scraps of homespun fabric, for little girls to play with.

The characteristic simplicity and harmonious materials of Shaker style allow the traditional Shaker dining room to fit into any period home. Rich glossy woods and classic lines fit well into Victorian terraces, yet the lack of embellishment and lightweight look mean this style would not overpower the most uncompromising modern home, however limited the space. The basic Shaker furniture is still very much available, some of which is made to original Shaker designs; there are also many new ranges that emulate their design and ethics. Many of the accessories too, such as white china and checked linens, are so classic they are perennially available. So the bright, harmonious Shaker dining room is within the reach of everyone.

$\mathcal{P}$ROJECTS

TAPE-WOVEN STOOL SEAT

The Shakers used coloured tapes that they had hand-loomed themselves to make comfortable stool and chair seats and sometimes backs. It is not difficult to weave a chair seat yourself, given a little practice and patience. If you start with a simple square stool , roll up the lengths of the tape before you start, and keep the tape taut as you go, you should quickly become accomplished and able to tackle more complicated designs.

45

You will need
❋

- Square-topped post and rung stool frame
- 8 small carpet tacks
- 2.5cm (1in) thick foam pad, cut to fit the inside dimensions of the stool seat
- Woven tape
- Tape measure
- Large safety pin or bodkin
- Blunt knife

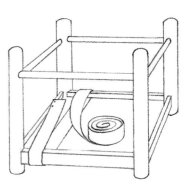

2 *Turn the stool upside-down and, starting from the left hand stretcher, turn the end of the tape under and put one tack about 1cm (½ in) from the back left post Pull the tape over the front stretcher and around to the back stretcher. Then put in another tack just in front of the first.*

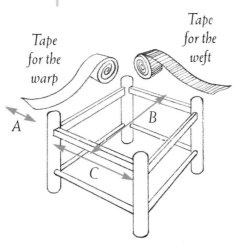

Tape for the warp

Tape for the weft

A

B

C

1 *First calculate the quantity of tape you need. Start by measuring the width of the tape (A), either in imperial or metric, then keep to the same unit throughout your calculations. Measure around the stool rungs from front to back (B – warp). Measure the length of the front rung (C) and divide it by the width of the tape (A). Multiply this figure by the warp measurement you took (B). This will give you the amount of tape needed for the warp. Add a little extra – about 7.5cm (3in). Repeat the operation for the weft (side to side).*

3 *Keeping the tape taut, wind it from back to front until the stool seat is covered.*

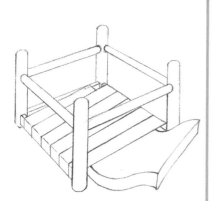

4 *Turn the tape under and tack it into position about 1 cm (½ in) from the front stretcher. Ease the foam in between the upper and lower tapes.*

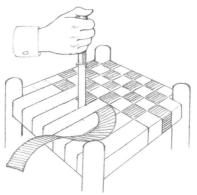

6 *Weave along the first 'row' of the top side, then pull the tape taut, using the blunt knife to tighten the row, then turn the stool over and weave along the top side.*

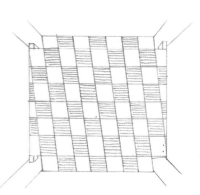

7 *Continue like this until the seat is completely woven. Tack the tape under the last warp.*

5 *Turn the stool upside-down with the back nearest you and, using a contrast colour for the weft (side to side), tack it in place under the left-hand warp tape. Fix a large safety pin or bodkin to the end of the tape then, keeping the tape taut, weave it over and under the warp tapes.*

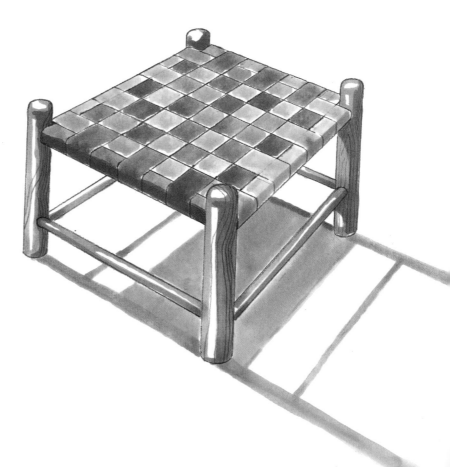

HEART CROSS STITCH LINENS

Although Shakers were exhorted by Mother Ann Lee not to embellish anything, they did produce high quality goods to sell to the outside world, and many of these would have been embroidered. The heart motif was particularly favoured as it signified offering their hearts to God. Worked in cross stitch, it is extremely easy to lend delightful yet discreet decoration to table linen, bed linen, cushions, and even children's clothes.

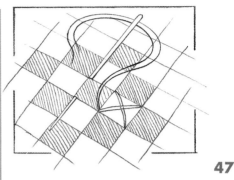

You will need
❋

- Linens to be embroidered – preferably with a thick even weave, or with a fine checked pattern
- Stranded embroidery thread to contrast
- Needle
- Embroidery scissors

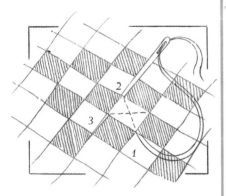

1 *The neatest way to do cross stitch is by working the crosses over a set number of threads in the fabric to be embroidered, or by working on finely checked fabrics, which give a framework for each cross. Work from right to left and use either two or three strands of thread, depending on the weight of the fabric. Bring the threaded needle up through the fabric at the bottom right-hand corner of the*

first cross (1), take it down at the top left (2) and thread it up to the right side of the fabric again at the bottom left (3).

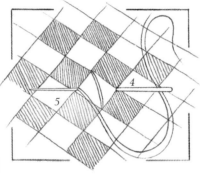

2. *Bring the thread across the first stitch, down at the top right (4) to complete the first cross. Then bring the needle to the right side of the fabric again at the bottom right of the next stitch (5).*

3. *Take the needle down at the top left and out again at the bottom left, ready to finish off the second cross at the top right. Make sure all the top stitches of the cross go in the same direction.*

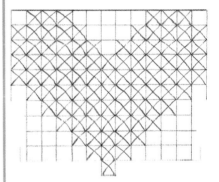

4. *Working from the diagram, starting at the bottom and counting the stitches as you go, complete the heart motif.*

CHAPTER FIVE

*L*IVING ROOMS

THE NEED FOR A HARMONIOUS OASIS in which to unwind after running the gauntlet of the pace of modern life must surely have become greater as our lifestyles have become faster. There is a yearning among many of us to shut our doors at the end of the day and relax in peaceful calm surroundings, uncluttered by the distracting 'sophistication' of pattern, adornment and loud colours. Although the Shakers themselves did not have living rooms – rather meeting rooms in which they would congregate for prayer, contemplation and social gatherings – by taking inspiration from their style and philosophy, we can benefit from surroundings whose harmony runs much deeper than looks. Their style and their designs

1 *Walls painted in Shaker blues and greens*
2 *Unembellished fireplace*
3 *Built-in cupboards with simple panels and small wooden knobs*
4 *Metal candlesticks*
5 *Tin wall sconces*
6 *Metal pendant candelabra*
7 *Pine floorboards*
8 *Woven wool matting*
9 *Green checked fabric for upholstery*
10 *Shaker-style woollen throw*
11 *Peg rail*
12 *Pedestal table*
13 *Windsor chair*
14 *Split cane basket*

all have a spiritual quality, born of years of perfecting the lines, balance, and proportions as a form of worship.

FABRICS

The most obvious ingredient missing from Shaker living areas that is an important ingredient of a modern living room is upholstery. But, by taking on the general Shaker design philosophy, it is not difficult to find sofas and chairs that would sit happily in a Shaker-style living room. Look for smooth, flowing outlines that neither have a rigid boxy modern look, nor are cluttered with fiddly twirls or carving. For covers, select typical Shaker-style fabrics in smudgy greens or blues, ox-blood reds or soft yellow ochres. Plain fabric would be very much in keeping and, with numerous current ranges offering a wide choice of shades, it should not be difficult to find exactly what you want. Alternatively, choose a checked fabric to offer unfussy relief to plain surroundings.

Curtains, too, could be either plain or checked, though stripes are in keeping with the Shaker preference for unfussy geometrics. Drapes should have loop headings which demand neither gathering nor pleating, and can be used to hook onto the peg rail as well as metal curtain rails. Another fabric you can use in your living room is a rug, either striped in woven wool or, possibly, a rag rug.

WALLS

The walls should be plain and, although the Shaker preference was for white, you can introduce more colour while still retaining the Shaker look by using shades from their colour palette. North-facing rooms will benefit from the warmer shades, such as buffed yellow ochres, soft greens and olives. South- and west-facing rooms can come alive with mellow bluish-greens or greenish-blues. But whatever shades you choose, for the instantly recognizable Shaker look, fix a peg rail around the walls. You can either leave it as natural wood or paint it, together with the rest of the woodwork in the room, to contrast and tone in with the walls in any of the above tones or a rich earthy ox-blood red.

Opposite: Make Shaker-style curtains from checked fabrics and hang them on metal rails. This modern rail finishes with a simple graceful curve which is pleasing to the eye, yet shows no unnecessary embellishment, a detail of which the Brethren and Sisters would surely have approved.

Efficient built-in storage becomes a delight to the eye when finely finished and detailed. It provides visual interest to walls, making a backdrop here to a candle table and Shaker rocking chair.

STORAGE

When choosing storage for your living room, choose in-built cupboards. Alcoves on either side of a chimney breast offer an ideal opportunity for building in storage, and if you have them built from floor to ceiling, just as the Shakers did, you will exclude any dust traps and cut down on daily cleaning.

Cabinets and other wooden furniture in keeping with Shaker style are not difficult to find. The Shakers designed and made a wide range of wooden chairs, settles, side tables and candle tables. Many of their original designs are still produced today, and other manufacturers have also been able to draw inspiration from Shakers in their own designs. Simple wooden country furniture would not be out of place, either. For example, although most of the genuine Shaker chairs were ladder-back, the Brethren and Sisters would have been familiar with other farmhouse style chairs such as Windsor. Mother Ann Lee, herself, took one with her to America, and it was subsequently fitted with American-style rockers.

A graceful reproduction Shaker candle table shows the typical smooth arching curves of the pedestal feet. Made from solid cherry wood, it would make an elegant lamp table today.

SHAKER BOXES

Although the Shaker-style living room should not contain any unnecessary ornamentation, you can display a range of Shaker boxes. These elegant oval boxes are made of wood with tapering finger-like joins which are beautifully fixed in place with perfect lines of copper tacks. The Shakers made them in many sizes and painted them in their favourite muted shades. Stack them on shelves, where they can be used to store all manner of small and fiddly things, as well as offering visual interest in wonderful harmonious shades.

The design and making of these Shaker boxes is a testament to Shaker lifestyle in every way. The Shakers' orderly lives demanded a practical flexible storage system, so they adopted a classic box design that had been made in England for about 100 years. The original English design was almost round; the finger-like swallowtail joins were fewer per box and more angular. The Shakers gradually

This simple tinware, designed on lines that are pleasing in their simplicity, is not dissimilar to goods the Shakers themselves would have used. They make delightful, authentic accessories for a modern living room.

Elegant, oval wooden boxes with refined swallowtail joins have become an icon of Shaker style. Painted in the muted shades of nature with pigments derived from local plants and clays, they have a universal appeal. Filled with smaller everyday needs, they will bring order to your life; stacked high on shelves, they will become a visual delight.

changed the proportions of the basic box, elongating it into an elegant oval and streamlining the swallowtails to turn what was the everyday storage equivalent of the tin cannister into a visual treat. But the changes were not all visual. With their inbuilt sense of quality and practicality, the Shakers made boxes that would best withstand the vagaries of the New England winters by carefully selecting the timber and adjusting the joins. The sides of the box were made from maple, a local hardwood that, once steamed or soaked in hot water, could easily be bent around the moulds. However, as hardwoods like maple expand in wet weather, the Shaker Elders chose the more stable softwood pine for the tops and bottoms of their boxes as it was less likely to buckle when conditions got damp. The swallowtail joins were also designed to cope with damp conditions as they left more room for the wood to swell and shrink than if they had been straight.

By 1798, these beautiful Shaker boxes, painted in deep smudgy shades, were being sold to the outside world. They were expensive even then, but valued for their workmanship and quality that ensured they lasted for years of daily use. Just 50 years later, however, these boxes were less in demand. They were displaced by the new and cheaper tin cannisters that were now being turned out by 'whitesmiths' who had discovered the versatility of the new rolled tin. So the Shaker Brethren turned to a different market. By giving the boxes a handle, lining them with brocade and equipping them with a handmade tomato or strawberry pincushion and a needlecase, they were sold as needlework baskets.

ACCESSORIES

In addition to these classic oval boxes, you can include metal candle-holders in your living room. Choose from metal candelabra, simple candlesticks, candle-holders to hang on a peg rail, and elegant tin sconces and lanterns. Arrange them either singly or in decorative groups.

A peg rail offers ample scope for decorative detail in a Shaker-style living room. In addition to candle-holders, you can hang a

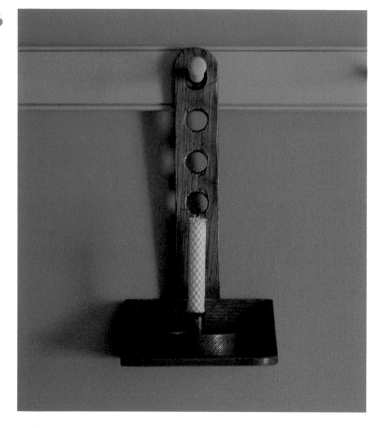

traditional broomcorn hand-brush alongside candle-boxes, coats, hats, small cupboards and even ladder-back chairs. To give the living room a natural appeal, you may also like to hang garlands of dried herbs, herbal rings or herbal sachets on the peg rail, all of which make an ever-changing picture on the wall at the same time as providing a fresh aroma.

For a truly Shaker feel, as the sun goes down, light the candles, and supplement these with lanterns placed on small circular candle tables, or, if you have children or pets, hang them on the peg rail. However, while this creates a wonderful atmosphere when you are entertaining, if you are relaxing *en famille* in the evening, reading or watching television, you will need the benefit of electric light. Choose your lighting by following the Shakers' own philosophy of well-designed, simple lights free from embellishment. The most suitable would probably be simple lights on metal stands teamed with parchment-coloured shades, a combination of materials and colours that would be at home in a Shaker dwelling house.

Current trends in home decoration have a compatibility with Shaker styles: there is an abundance of wooden furniture built on clean lines available; as well as plenty of checked fabrics, wrought iron curtain rails, door furniture and accessories, plus tinware sconces and lanterns. So, even though the Shakers did not actually have living rooms, it will not be difficult, once you have the basic structure in place, to create a delightful, relaxing space that even the Brethren and Sisters would have been comfortable in.

Adding a peg rail to a room immediately stamps it with Shaker style. If you want to add more colour to a white room, choose from the classic Shaker palette. The Brethren and Sisters themselves would have preferred to paint just the woodwork and peg rail, but you can add a little of your own style by painting the walls in a colour from the palette, too. Shades of blue and green were much favoured.

PROJECTS

LOOP-HEADED CURTAINS

The Shaker Sisters sewed loops to the tops of all their curtains and wall cloths so that they could be either threaded through metal poles or hung on the peg rail. It is a simple, visually pleasing hanging system that requires little more than a needle and thread and, of course, fabric. With no need for tapes, hooks, fussy gathering or pleating, it fitted comfortably with their philosophy of beauty in utility. Yet this deceptively simple method offers delightfully practical and elegant finished results.

You will need

- Fabric for window (see step 1)
- Tape measure
- Scissors
- Needle and thread

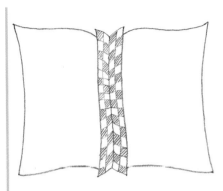

2 *With right sides together and patterns matching from the top, stitch the widths together for each curtain. Press the seams open.*

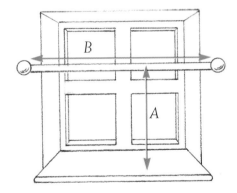

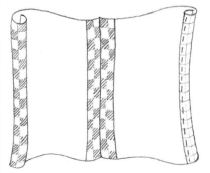

3 *Turn in and stitch a double hem at both sides of each curtain. Press.*

1 *First calculate your fabric needs. Measure the length from the curtain track to the windowsill or floor (A), depending on your choice of style, and add on 25cm (10in) for turnings. This figure will need to be multiplied by the number of fabric widths (drops) needed to cover the window. Calculate the number of drops by measuring the width of the curtain track (B) and multiplying this by two, then dividing by the width of the fabric. For each loop, allow a strip of fabric 10 x 20cm (4 x 8in). You will need one loop per 20cm (8in) along the width of the curtain. Cut the fabric into the calculated lengths. If you have an even number of drops, for example four, you will be able to use complete widths for each window. If you have an odd number, for example three, one drop will have to be cut in half lengthwise to make curtains of equal widths.*

continued over ➤

4 *Turn up and baste a generous double hem at the bottom edge. Stitch and press.*

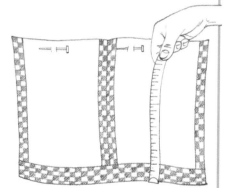

5 *Check the curtain length by measuring up from the bottom in three places along the width of the curtain, and mark each place with a pin. Turn down the top of the curtain by about 2.5cm (1in) below this mark (this will allow for the length of the loops) and baste in position.*

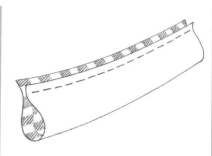

6 *To make the loops, fold each piece of fabric cut for the loops in half lengthwise, with right sides facing. Stitch along the length. Trim the seam, then turn the fabric right way out.*

7 *Turn in the ends and slip stitch them together to neaten.*

8 *Baste or pin the loops to the back of the curtain at 20cm (8in) intervals, 4cm (1½in) from the top. Stitch along the whole width of the curtain near the top, taking in the loops. Sew another line of stitches along the width of the curtain to take in the bottom edges of the loops.*

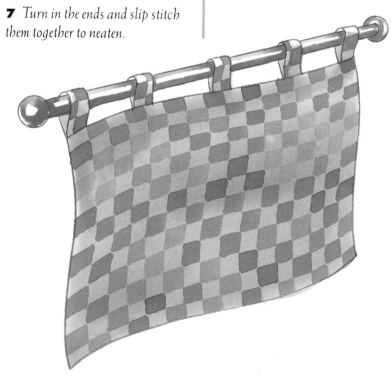

APPLIQUED HEART CUSHION

This delightful cushion made from homespun fabric features an appliquéd heart with a tiny pearl button detail. It is very easy to make as the appliquéd shape is frayed at the edges, dispensing with the need for fiddly turning in. The heart shape was a popular motif that appeared on many items the Shakers made for sale to the outside world. To them, it signified 'Heart to God'; universally, it is an emblem signifying love and welcome.

4 Snip all four corners and press the seams open.

You will need
❋

- 1m (1yd) checked cotton fabric
- Stranded embroidery thread to contrast with fabric
- Scissors
- Tracing paper
- Soft pencil
- Needle and thread
- Small pearl button
- Small cushion pad, 25cm (10in) square

2 Using the same stranded embroidery thread, sew the button to the dip in the heart.

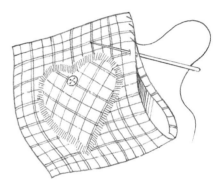

5 Turn the cushion right side out and insert the cushion pad. Turn in the edges of the open side and slip stitch them together to close.

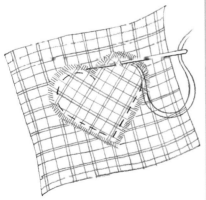

1 Cut two squares of fabric measuring 30cm (12in) square. Trace off a heart motif and use this to cut out the heart shape in fabric on the bias. Fray the edges of the heart shape. Baste it onto the right side of one fabric square. Using three strands of embroidery thread, sew the heart motif to the fabric square using running stitch.

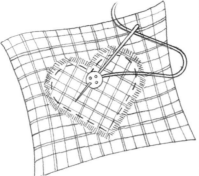

3 Place the fabric pieces right sides together and stitch around three sides, leaving one side open.

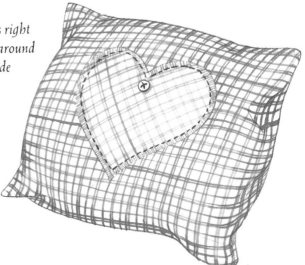

CHAPTER SIX

KITCHENS

IN EVERY HOME, THE KITCHEN MUST BE the most hardworking room. It is a store, a factory for family food and very often a dining and living room too. The demands on a kitchen are immense in that it needs to be both efficient and welcoming. Shaker kitchens certainly had to be efficient as they had to cater for three meals a day for up to 100 Brethren and Sisters. Those working in the kitchen also had to make time for making butter and cheese every day and, during the summer and autumn, time for preserving produce from the garden: making jams and pickles, drying beans, fruits and vegetables, and salting and drying meat. To ensure this efficiency, the Shakers developed several systems that we find work in our kitchens today: ample built-in storage cupboards to provide dust- and grease-free housing for equipment, utensils and crockery,

1 *Built-in cupboards with simple panels and knob handles*
2 *Wooden worktops*
3 *Large table with drawer*
4 *Wall-hung cupboard containing simple white china*
5 *Panelled door with wrought iron door furniture*
6 *Natural stone floor*
7 *Peg rail*
8 *Brass taps*

This modern kitchen island work-table made in elm with olive-painted drawer fronts has the simple lines and pleasing proportions that would have met with Shaker approval.

The fine, unembellished workmanship of this modern kitchen drawer (right) shows all the hallmarks of Shaker ideals. The clean design is beautifully finished with details such as rounded edges, and a worktop made of bias-laminated timber. Although this bias lamination is not entirely necessary, it does not interfere with the function of the worktop, yet greatly improves the look.

teamed with clear work areas and a range of ovens to provide for flexible cooking. They used a combination of a range for slow cooking, baking and frying, and spits for roasting. Even today, we can install ranges, such as those made by Aga or Rayburn; for fast cooking, we are more likely to choose a microwave oven.

This range in an authentic Shaker kitchen, is nevertheless a little ornate for their usual tastes. Their own designs would not have incorporated the decorative relief and curved feet.

STORAGE

There are plenty of built-in kitchen units to choose from today. To emulate the Shaker look, choose simple, panelled wooden units free from unnecessary moulding as these only serve to trap dust and grease. They can either be left as natural wood, varnished for protection, or painted in one of the deep muted Shaker shades such as olive, ochre, denim or turquoise blue, ox-blood red or greenish-blue. Many Shaker kitchens also had open shelves for storing mixing bowls or other crockery. You can either put up wall shelves and paint them the same colour as the units, or fix up shelf units in suitable Shaker shades.

Hanging shelves (below) painted in ox-blood red, a typical Shaker colour, provide practical storage while offering visual interest. Fine traditional wooden country chairs like this one (below right), would have been brought by folk when they joined Shaker communities. Its tall back, ample moulded seat and generously curved arms would all have contributed to comfort, while the fine proportions ensure that it is visually pleasing.

This corner of a kitchen (right) shows delightfully practical touches, such as the knife block and colander hanging on the peg rail. The stone sink, white walls and natural timber are also classic Shaker features.

The ubiquitous Shaker peg rail ran around kitchen walls, just as it did in every other room. Here, it was used for hanging utensils – in your own kitchen, you can also hang up mugs, cups and pans.

FURNITURE

Although the Shakers did not spend time sitting around in the kitchen – they were far too busy catering for meals – the few chairs they had would have been wooden country chairs – perhaps ladder-backs or Windsor-style chairs. Certainly, if you use the kitchen for eating as well as for food preparation, wooden chairs free from too much fancy fretwork or turning would fit very well.

WALLS AND FLOORS

Keeping to the Shaker colour schemes should work well in most kitchens. For an authentic look choose plain white walls and natural woodwork. Although ceramic tiles did not exist in the Shaker age, they are a practical solution in wet areas and, for that reason, if you wished to use them they would not go against the Shaker philosophy of function first. Choose plain tiles – either white, cream, or perhaps a terracotta that would team with the woodwork. Natural floors are also practical in the kitchen. The Shakers used flagstones made from local material; nowadays, there is a wider choice more readily available to us. Flagstones, quarry tiles or even a sheet flooring are acceptable floor coverings. The most suitable sheet flooring is linoleum, which is made from natural materials: a hessian or jute base coated with a mixture of powdered cork, linseed oil and pigment. Its natural quality means it will work well with the rest of the kitchen; it is easy to keep clean and less wearing on the feet than hard stone.

For wet areas, the Shakers made basic but efficient choices. Sinks were stone, taps and piping were copper, neither chromed nor covered up. The modern equivalent of the stone sink is a traditional ceramic sink. The Shakers would have approved of both its design and its practicality. Its simple square form offers no embellishment; the depth means plenty of room for washing without overflow and, being made of white ceramic, it does not scratch, retaining its clean looks for many years. Nowadays, we would probably choose to conceal the pipework, and certainly that would be very much in keeping as the result is streamlined looks, and less fiddly cleaning. The choice of brass taps would be both appealing and authentic.

FABRICS

The Shakers did not have curtains in their kitchens for two reasons. First, being within their own community, the kitchen would not have been overlooked by strangers and there was no demand for modesty in a kitchen, so there was no need for them. Second, curtains would have collected grease and dust. However, the

Opposite: This attractive modern kitchen, with its ceramic Butler sink, olive green-painted cupboards, hanging plate rack and stone floor, demonstrates the pure and simple lines that the Shakers would have chosen for their own.

The old Shakers would never have seen a modern domestic kitchen like this one, but it is practical for family living today and it demonstrates some of the Shaker ideals. The Aga cooker is a readily available modern range, similar to the ranges the Shakers used. The flush-fronted drawers with knob-pulls and plain panelled cupboards are the modern equivalent to Shaker storage, and the room is furnished with simple table and traditional country chairs.

Shakers did include cloths for covering and drying in their kitchen. These were woven from linen and cotton, and they were often a checked design, probably in blue and white. This most perennial of combinations is always a delight and will look fresh and attractive in any kitchen. Even now, blue and white checked tea towels are universally available, and could even be used imaginatively to make Shaker-style curtains. Sew on some white loops, then hook these onto cup hooks at the window and you will have a cheerful treatment that is very much in keeping with Shaker style.

ACCESSORIES

Shaker kitchen equipment would have included simple ceramic mixing bowls, large wooden bowls for proving dough in, wooden spoons and paddles, iron saucepans and kettles, tin bakeware and baskets for storing produce. All these offer wonderful visual appeal and can be used today to give your kitchen a Shaker personality. Even if you do not live anywhere near a Shaker community, it is possible to pick up old country kitchen utensils and equipment from car boot sales, antique fairs and bric-a-brac shops almost everywhere.

If you keep the Shaker philosophy of 'beauty in utility' in mind when choosing accessories, you will not go far wrong. A well-balanced pan is so much easier to use than an ill-balanced one; the fact that it looks more beautiful too is a treat. Before you buy anything, pick it up and try it out using the actions you may need for that particular piece of equipment. If it feels right, it is worth buying. Next, look at the design. Does it have any fussy detailing or embellishments that are unnecessary and clutter the basic lines? Very often, it is those items with clumsy designs that depend on distracting decoration to make them look reasonable. Smooth lines and good workmanship

Traditional ceramic mixing bowls set out on open shelves in a Shaker kitchen.

This country two-piece dresser, designed on simple lines and painted in a typical Shaker yellow, would sit happily in a Shaker-style kitchen. New Shakers may have brought furniture similar to this with them when they joined the community, although pieces they subsequently made would have had plainer wooden knob-pulls on the drawers.

need no covering up. By choosing only good plain everyday kitchen items (which need be no more 'sophisticated' than a well-loved traditional design), and putting them on display on shelves or a peg rail in the areas where they will be used, you can immediately create a cosy homely feel in keeping with the Shaker philosophy. You may like to include traditional wooden spoons, butter-coloured mixing bowls, and a simple iron skillet. Or you may choose a traditional hob kettle rather than an electric one if you have a range. Quite apart from the fact that the non-electric look is more in keeping with Shaker design, the flat-bottomed kettle demonstrates the Shaker philosophy that the function of the item must dictate the design. Its wide bottom increases the amount of water in contact with the heat, and so speeds up the boiling.

$\mathcal{P}$ROJECTS

HERBAL WREATH

The Shakers had large kitchen gardens which included extensive areas set aside for growing herbs. The herbs were used fresh in cooking and then dried to sell, or to make herbal gifts. This herbal wreath is made from fresh herbs, which give a wonderfully abundant look, and would make a delightful gift for any enthusiastic cook. The wreath is made up of the more woody-stemmed herbs, so it should stay fresh for a few days if it is sprayed with water regularly. Once it starts to wilt, take it apart and hang the bunches of herbs up to dry for flavouring dishes in the coming months.

71

You will need

✳

- Approximately 40 bay leaves
- Reel of florist's wire
- Large bunch of sage
- Large bunch of thyme
- Large bunch of parsley
- Large bunch of lavender
- Bunch of young rosemary shoots
- Hot glue gun and glue sticks
- Willow wreath base, about 30cm (12in) in diameter
- Raffia

2 *Wire up all the other herbs into small bunches.*

1 *Remove the bay leaves from their branches and, taking six leaves at a time, wind florist's wire around the stems to make small bunches.*

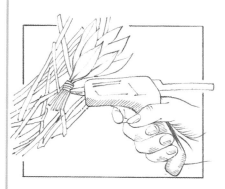

3 *Using the glue gun and hot glue sticks, stick a bunch of bay leaves onto the wreath.*

continued over ➤

4 *Affix the other herb bunches in turn, leaving aside the lavender, until the willow wreath is covered.*

5 *Tie each bunch of lavender with raffia and make a bow.*

6 *Arrange the lavender bunches evenly around the wreath, and when you are satisfied with the arrangement, glue them into position.*

TWIGGY HEART

The Shakers loved all things natural, and many of the items they made to sell to the outside world were fashioned from materials within the village. This twig heart is easy to make and would be a delightful accessory for any living room, whether hung on a peg rail, stood on a shelf or fixed to the wall. The Shakers were fond of the heart emblem, so it will immediately give a Shaker feel to any room.

You will need
❋

- 1.5m (5ft) heavy gauge metal wire
- Finer wire for binding
- Wire cutters
- 12 freshly cut fine branches, about 50cm (20in) long
- Secateurs

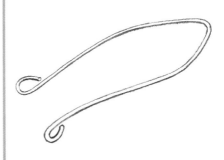

1 *Cut off 1m (3 ¼ ft) of the wire and bend one end into a loop, twisting the end to secure. Bend the other end to make a hook.*

2 *Form this piece of wire into a heart shape and hook the hooked end into the loop to secure.*

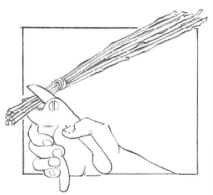

3 *Divide the twigs into two bundles. Bind the thick end of each bundle with wire. Trim these ends with secateurs.*

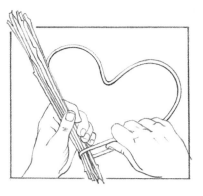

4 *Bind the end of one bundle to the bottom of the wire heart.*

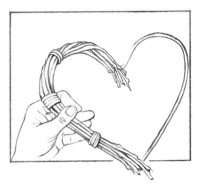

5 *Bind the twigs to the wire heart at intervals up one side of the heart shape until you reach the top. Repeat on the other side with the other bundle.*

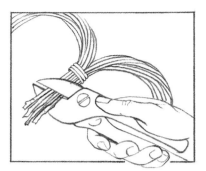

6 *Gather together all the twigs from the two bundles where they meet at the dip in the middle of the heart. Then bind them together with wire, and fix them to the wire shape. Trim the ends to neaten.*

CHAPTER SEVEN

Bedrooms

IN REALITY, SHAKERS DID NOT HAVE private bedrooms. Living a communal celibate lifestyle, they slept in dormitory-like retiring rooms of four to five Brethren or Sisters to a room; they each had a chair, a bed, a strip of carpet and storage space.

However, nothing could be easier than creating a harmonious bedroom, restful in its simplicity, yet efficient in its planning, using the basic elements of Shaker design. Start with the basics of white walls, peg rail, built-in storage and a simple rug on varnished floorboards, then add the furnishings.

FABRICS

For our tastes, Shaker furnishings were rudimentary: wooden beds and homespun fabrics, very often in blue and white check for curtains and bedclothes. The Sisters would have chosen the simplest

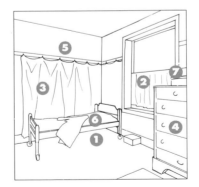

1 *Simple wooden bed*
2 *White loop-headed curtains*
3 *Checked loop-headed wall cloth*
4 *Wooden chest with gradated drawers and wooden knobs*
5 *Peg rail*
6 *Blue bedclothes*
7 *Shaker boxes for storage*

Three different blue and white checks, layered one upon the other, lend a welcoming warmth to rudimentary stripped floors and white walls, amply demonstrating the ease with which these geometrics can be mixed.

look possible but, nowadays, it can be enriched by piling check on check, appliquéing one to another or using complementary checks as borders or trims. The glorious thing about decorating using checked fabrics is that you cannot go wrong. Mix the sizes – small check with large for a feeling of depth – either choosing them all in one colour or teaming two or more together. The colours in the classic Shaker palette are so harmonious they can be mixed and matched at will. Use them for curtains, bedclothes and cushions for a fresh coordinated look.

*Varying sizes of checks in typical
Shaker shades look fabulous when
teamed together, combining colour
schemes that are easy to live with,
and failsafe pattern coordination.*

For bedding, the Shakers used sheets and woollen blankets. Unlike many of the other European groups coming to America from Europe, they were not known for their quilt making. This is probably because their founder, Mother Ann Lee, started her working life as a textile worker in Manchester, England; with so much cloth being woven in the area, there was no need to make patchwork from scraps. If they had made quilts, they would certainly not have opted for the more flamboyant designs made from shaped pieces and decorated with appliqué. If you would like to include a quilt in your Shaker bedroom, opt for simple square patches in unfussy geometric fabrics, perhaps arranged chequerboard or herringbone fashion to create a similar effect to Shaker seats.

STORAGE

From a practical point of view, the Shakers were great champions of plenty of built-in storage. It was not uncommon to see a whole wall banked with cupboards and up to 860 drawers, stretching from floor to ceiling. In essence, this is very similar to modern bedroom storage yet, by emulating the Shaker designs, you can recreate their distinctive harmonious mood. The cupboards and drawers were built in different sizes to suit their intended contents, ranging from boxy square drawers with a knob set in the centre, to generous and elegant long drawers with a pair of knobs. A chest could consist of seemingly endless drawers, all of the same size, or it might have drawers gradated in depth from top to bottom. The top drawers were often smaller and narrower, while the bottom ones tended to be larger for heavier contents. But, whatever the design, the knobs were always placed in perfect serried ranks for a uniformed look.

Usually left in natural wood tones, the storage systems would give a warming golden glow right across the room. It was not unusual for them to be painted, however, which offers more flexible colour scheming for modern decorators in the Shaker style. Keeping to the classic palette, you can create soft warm rooms by coordinating the cupboards and fabric choices. Blues were a firm Shaker favourite, though these can look cold in north-facing rooms. For them, you may like to choose the warmer yellow ochres.

ACCESSORIES

Nowadays, you can make your Shaker bedroom rather cosier than the original Shaker retiring rooms by accessorizing with some of the everyday items the Brethren and Sisters may have had around them elsewhere in the dwelling houses. They would certainly condone the use of their fine baskets made of oak and ash splint. The Shakers

Opposite: Walls of storage such as this provide a perfect practical solution for bedrooms where, nowadays, space is at a premium. The Shakers built flexible systems, allowing for different depths of drawers by gradating them so that the deeper drawers were at the bottom, and narrower ones were at the top, for a visually pleasing effect. The wooden knob-pulls were always arranged in perfect lines for unity.

favoured well-proportioned, gracefully shaped baskets that were lightweight yet deceptively strong. They made their baskets from splints of black ash which they obtained by first removing the bark, then pounding the log from one end to the other until one year's growth began to separate. It could take days for all the growth rings to be pounded off the log. The splints then had to be divided in half lengthways to expose the satin sheen of the inner wood which was cleaned by scraping it with a knife and then finely sanding it. Finally, the strips were cut to the desired width for that particular design of basket. It was only then that the Shakers were ready to start weaving. The baskets were woven damp around wooden moulds, which were also made by the Shakers. The Brethren usually made the larger baskets for outdoor work and laundry, while the Sisters made fine sewing baskets and other small baskets for indoor use. When finished, the ash baskets were almost white in colour, although they soon mellowed down into the rich golden shades they are still known for today.

These baskets look highly decorative nowadays in a bedroom, while also providing useful storage space for sewing kits, hair accessories, and even make-up. All shapes and sizes were made by the Shakers. One of the most popular was the cathead – so called because when you turn it upside-down, it looks like the head of a cat. They also made elegant lidded baskets and, being highly practical, they often designed the lid to be attached permanently to the handle so it could not get lost.

Other decorative yet Shaker-inspired detailing you can use in the bedroom include handmade rag dolls dressed in country style clothes made of homespun fabric. The Shakers made these for the children they looked after, who either joined the community when their parents became Shakers, or who were rescued from broken families. Although the Shakers never used any plants or flowers for decorative purposes as this would have been seen as frivolous, you can use lavender bags for scenting drawers or hanging from the peg rail to create a sweetly scented ambience.

PROJECTS

LAVENDER POTS

These charming arrangements of dried lavender in terracotta pots, tied around with raffia, make delightful bedroom decorations; not only are they appealing to look at, they also smell nice. You could make one, or several to arrange in lines or groups on shelves. They are incredibly easy to put together and other dried flowers, such as roses, can be added to ring the changes.

You will need
✽

- Dry florist's foam (small cones work well)
- Small clay pot
- Bunch of dried lavender
- Knife
- Short length of raffia
- Scissors
- Glue gun and glue sticks (optional)

2 *Cut the lavender stalks to the right height for the pot. Insert the lavender into the foam so that it is packed tightly.*

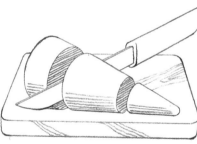

1 *Using a knife, cut the dry foam to fit the pot. If you are using a cone, cut the top off where the circumference fits the bottom of the pot, then cut further up to fit the pot. Place the foam in the pot.*

ONE-PATCH QUILT

A one-patch quilt is so-called because each block is made up of only one patch, rather than several pieces (often of varying shapes) stitched together to form a design block. It is the simplest form of patchwork, and therefore the best introduction to this absorbing and popular craft. By using simple geometric fabrics you can make up delightful designs, like this one using stripes in alternating directions. Patchwork is very exacting as it will only fit together well if you cut out and stitch the pieces accurately. However, with care, it is not difficult to do. The combination of this simple design and the need for precision fits exactly with the Shaker ideals.

You will need

❋

- 3m (3 yd 9in) striped cotton fabric
- 2m (2yd 6in) sheeting for backing, or equivalent in another fabric, 2m (2yd 6in) wide
- 2m (2 yd 6in) square of medium-weight polyester wadding (batting)
- 2.5m (3yd) fabric for binding
- Thin card
- Soft pencil
- Ruler
- Scissors
- Pins
- Sewing machine
- Sewing thread
- Tape measure
- Needle

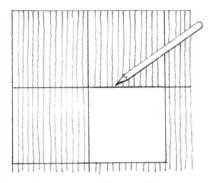

1 On a piece of thin card, draw out an accurate square measuring 21cm (8¼ in) square. Cut the fabric into four equal pieces. Pull a thread out at the cut end of each piece of the fabric to establish the grain and place the fabric wrong-side up on a large flat table. Position the template with one side along the selvedge, the other along the drawn thread. Using a soft pencil, draw around the template. Reposition the template so it butts up to the first position and draw around this. Continue until you have drawn out 100 squares.

3 Tie raffia around the rim of the pot. Secure with glue. A glue gun with hot melt wax works best.

continued over ➤

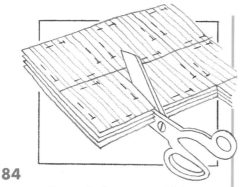

2 Layer the four pieces of fabric one on top of the other, lining up the drawn threads, with the marked-up piece on top. Pin the fabric together at regular intervals. Using sharp scissors, cut out the squares accurately.

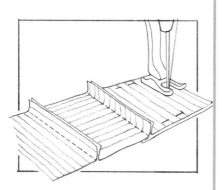

3 With right sides together and the stripes arranged so that they go in opposite directions, stitch two squares together, giving a seam allowance of exactly 5mm (¼ in). Continue to sew squares together with the stripes alternating until you have a strip of 20 squares. Make 20 similar strips, ensuring that half of the strips start with the stripes running horizontally, the other half with stripes running vertically.

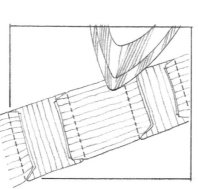

4 Press the seams to one side. Make sure that half of the strips have the seams going in one direction, the other half in the other direction. Stitch the strips together, making sure the stripes alternate. Press the seams to one side.

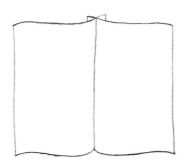

5 Make up the backing fabric to measure 2m (2yd 6in) square. If you are using sheeting, you may be able to buy it in 2m (2yd 6in) widths; if not, you may have to sew two or more narrower widths together.

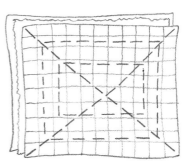

6 Sandwich the wadding (batting) between the backing fabric and the prepared patchwork top. Pin into position at the corners, then baste lines at intervals across and down the quilt to stop slipping while you bind the edges.

7 Roll the quilt up from corner to corner and slip the roll under the machine head so that the loose corner points outwards under the needle. Stitch diagonal lines across the quilt, unrolling it more with each line.

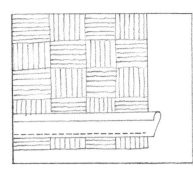

8 *Prepare the binding by cutting four strips of fabric, all 25cm (10in) wide. Two should measure 2m (2yd 6in) long and two 2.5m (2yd 20in) long. With right sides facing and raw edges together, stitch the shorter lengths to the top and bottom of the quilt. Turn the binding to the underside of the quilt and turn in 1cm (½in) hem and slip stitch into place.*

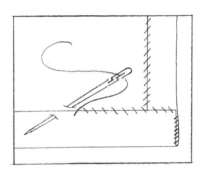

9 *With right sides together, stitch the longer pieces to the sides of the quilt so the ends extend beyond the binding at the top and bottom. Turn to the wrong side, turn in a 1cm (½in) hem and slip stitch into position. Trim to 1cm (½in) longer than the top and bottom binding, then turn this in and slip stitch to finish.*

CHAPTER EIGHT

ℬATHROOMS

ALTHOUGH SHAKER COMMUNITIES DID NOT include bathrooms, the Shakers themselves were meticulous about cleanliness.

'It is contrary to order for any slovens or sluts to live in the church, or even for Brethren or Sisters to wear ragged clothes around their work,' stated the Millenial Laws. So washing had to be thorough, and it took place every morning, night, and after work at the wash stand in the corner of the retiring room. True to Shaker ideals, this was usually made in plain wood, and was topped by a white china bowl and jug. The washing area was one place the Shakers allowed mirrors – usually hung from the peg rail, but they were never more than 30 x 45cm (12 x 18in) for fear that anyone may be tempted to vanity. This area, too, was one where curtains (usually loop-headed and made from white or homespun fabric) were demanded for modesty.

These elements can be incorporated into bathrooms today, providing a harmonious atmosphere for relaxing as well as washing.

1 *Wooden wash stand with jug and bowl*
2 *Peg rail with small mirror*
3 *White loop-headed curtains*
4 *White linen towels*
5 *Ladder-back chair with tape-woven seat*
6 *White walls*

The peg rail can be used for more than simply visual accessories. It provides the perfect storage solution in a bathroom that is too small to allow it permanent floor space for a chair. Always near at hand, it can be reached down when bathing or drying children. The tongue-and-groove also provides perfect housing for the toilet cistern in keeping with the Shaker ideal of cutting down on dust-gathering surfaces. Install a removable panel at the top for maintenance.

FURNITURE AND STORAGE

If the Shakers had had bathrooms, they would doubtless have chosen a pure white suite with brass taps (chroming adds cost), although since chrome taps are now deemed to be quite basic, perhaps they would have chosen a simple design in chrome.

A peg rail will immediately give the bathroom a Shaker signature, and it will, indeed, be very useful there. As well as hanging up typical Shaker belongings that we now see as decorative, we can hang up bags of bath toys for the children, towels, flannels, and even shampoo or gel designed with an integral hook for hanging in showers. You can also hang up a simple chair; this might be an invaluable way to store it, especially if the room is normally too small to allow space for a chair. In that way, the chair can be taken down only when it is needed.

The bathroom cabinet can also be hung Shaker-style from the peg rail, well away from young childrens' hands. Choose a simple wooden one, free from embellishment, with a wooden knob door-pull to fit with the Shaker style. You can then, perhaps, paint it to tone in with the rest of the room, to create a delightful, coordinated scheme.

WALLS

To give your bathroom a Shaker look, paint the walls white. Although Shakers did not have ceramic tiles, you can use these in Shaker colours in a bathroom today. Tongue-and-groove cladding is another good solution for wet areas of the bathroom; this can be painted in one of the colours from the Shaker palette. Choose a gloss or water-resistent vinyl paint from one of the kitchen and bathroom ranges, and paint each panel with one coat before fixing them together. Once fixed, paint on two more coats, allowing the first to dry thoroughly before applying the second. Seal joins between bath or basin and cladding with a waterproof mastic.

FABRICS

Coordinate a Shaker homespun fabric with the paint used for the cladding, and make a pair of simple loop-headed curtains to fit the window (see page 57). For extra interest, you can add a trim around the edges in a contrasting homespun fabric.

This modern bathroom has been inspired by Shaker style, with colour introduced by painting tongue-and-groove cladding in a favourite Shaker shade.

    Clean hands in Shaker times would have been dried on linen or cotton towels and, nowadays, it is delightful to incorporate a flat-woven towel such as these for guests, among the family terry towels in the bathroom. The Shakers probably would have hung their towels on a wooden clothes-horse, or even from a drying rail

Herbal garlands and nightdress-case dollies hang decoratively on the peg rail. The dollies provide a practical storage solution, while the herbs offer a sweet aroma, especially when the steam rises to release their perfume.

mounted onto the peg rail. A simple metal rail, perhaps chosen to match the curtain rail, is also in keeping, and can be teamed with a shorter version for a toilet roll holder.

ACCESSORIES

The room can be accessorized with wonderful everyday Shaker items, such as candle sconces, hand brushes, and baskets or stacked boxes, which could be filled with manicure kits, soaps or cotton wool. Another delightful touch is to hang up aromatic dried herb garlands which release their scent when they are dampened with steam. Other products inspired by the Shaker tradition that you can use and display in the bathroom include herbal soaps and bath milk grains.

PROJECTS

HAND IN HEART LAVENDER SACHET

The Shakers grew, dried and sold many herbal products, and this delightful lavender sachet illustrates many of their ideas. Made from homespun fabric, it is much more to their taste than the frilly Victorian styles; it is also appliquéd with an emblem that was symbolic to their lifestyle. The hand in heart for the Shakers signified hands to work and hearts to God. But even without those religious connotations, it is a motif that has universal meaning.

You will need

❉

- 30 x 15cm (12 x 6in) cotton fabric for each sachet
- Scissors
- Pins
- Needle
- Tape measure
- Tracing paper
- Soft pencil
- Contrasting fabric scraps for motifs
- Sewing thread to match heart and hand motifs
- Stranded embroidery thread to contrast with motifs
- Dried lavender, for filling

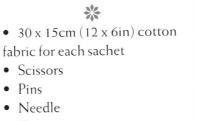

Template for heart motif

square. Next, prepare the motif patterns by using tracing paper and a soft pencil to trace hand and heart motifs. Cut these out. Use these patterns to cut motifs from contrasting fabric scraps.

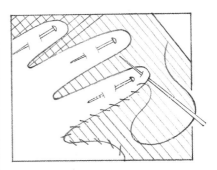

2 *Pin the hand motif to the front of one square of fabric. Carefully slip stitch this into position, turning the edges under as you go.*

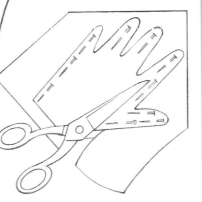

1 *For each sachet, cut two squares of fabric measuring 15cm (6in)*

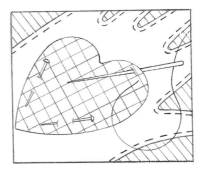

3 *Pin the heart shape on top of the hand motif and slip stitch this into position in the same way.*

continued over ➤

4 Using two strands of stranded embroidery thread in a colour that contrasts with the hand, embroider around the edge of the hand motif using tiny running stitches. Repeat around the heart motif.

6 Snip off all four corners. Press the seams open.

5 Place the sachet squares right sides together and stitch around the edges, leaving about 5cm (2in) unstitched.

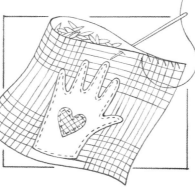

7 Turn the sachet the right way out and fill with dried lavender. Close the opening using slip stitch, turning the edges in as you go.

MUSLIN DRAWSTRING BATHBAGS

Relaxing or invigorating, real bath herbs need to be contained in fine muslin bags while their aroma is released by holding them under the hot water tap. Fill a jar with your chosen herbs: a mixture of camomile, hops and lime flowers for a relaxing bath, or basil, bay, rosemary, sage, thyme, lavender, lemon balm and lemon verbena for a stimulating bath. At bath time, put a small amount of the mixture into the bag, pull the drawstrings tight to close, then hang it on the hot tap as the bath runs. Afterwards, empty and wash the bag ready for the next bath.

You will need
❋

- 36 x 30cm (14 x 12in) muslin
- Needle and thread
- 2m (2yd 6in) ribbon
- Scissors
- Herbal bath mix

1 Turn in 7cm (2³⁄₄in) at each end of the muslin so that the right sides are together. Stitch, leaving 1cm (¼ in) unstitched at the hem edge for turning in later. Turn the right way out.

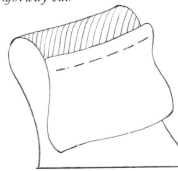

2 To make the casing, turn this whole stitched end back on itself. Turn in the raw edge, then stitch through all three layers.

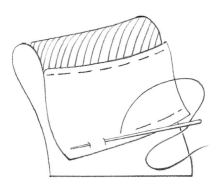

3 Stitch through all layers at the lower edge of the casing. Repeat at the other end.

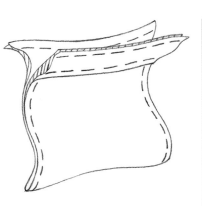

4 With right sides together, stitch the side seams, leaving the casing free. Turn the right way out.

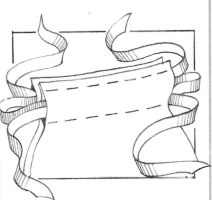

5 Cut the ribbon in half and thread one half through the casing. Thread the other half through the casing in the other direction.

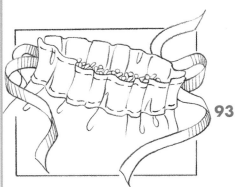

6 Fill the bag with bath herbs, pull the drawstrings to close the bag, then hang it over the hot tap as you run your bath so the water is infused with the herbs. Replace with fresh herbs for the next bath.

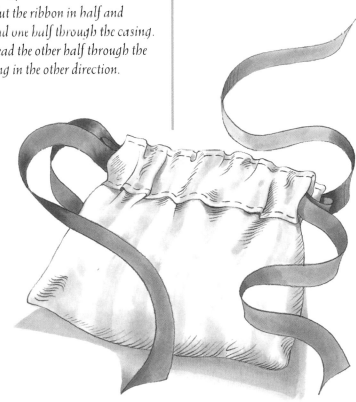

$\mathcal{I}$NDEX

ACKNOWLEDGEMENTS

Photographs courtesy of:

Appalachia – The Folk Art Shop: 01727 836796 pp.32, 55, 77, 90; Hancock Shaker Village/Richard Bryant/Arcaid p.33; Artisan Furniture & Accessories: 0171 498 6974 pp.21, 50; Camera Press/Avotakka p.43; Michael Freeman pp. 7,8, 11, 14, 18–9, 22, 26, 28–9, 36–7, 53, 54, 65, 74–5, 78, 86; Jan Baldwin/Country Homes & Interiors/Robert Harding Syndication p.44; Graham Rae/Ideal Home/Robert Harding Syndication p.76; James Merrell/Country Homes & Interiors/Robert Harding Syndication pp.48–9, 56; Hayloft Woodwork: 0181 747 3510 pp.41, 62(t), 66; Fritz von der Schulenburg/The Interior Archives: 0171 370 0595 pp.63, 69; Plain English: 01449 774028 pp.60–1; The Recollections Furniture Company: 01544 318092 pp.24, 27, 31, 39, 40, 52; Sanderson: 0171 584 3344 p.81; Somerset Creative Products: 01278 641622 p.64(l); Somerset House of Iron Ltd: 0171 371 0436 pp.64(r), 70; Andreas von Einsiedel/Elizabeth Whiting & Associates pp.88, 89; Woodstock Furniture Ltd: 0171 245 9989 pp.62(b), 68.